Tiny PIN-UPS:

Blondes!

SUSAN BERNARD

WARNER **W** TREASURES™
PUBLISHED BY WARNER BOOKS
A TIME WARNER COMPANY

*I have tried my very best to correctly identify
all my father's photographic subjects and apologize
if there is an error.*

Warner Books, Inc.,
1271 Avenue of the Americas
New York, NY 10020

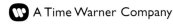 A Time Warner Company

Book design by Lisa C. McGarry

Printed in Mexico
First Printing: March 1995
10 9 8 7 6 5 4 3 2 1

ISBN:0-446-91003-1

For my son, Joshua Miller

The dazzling Blonde was an essential part of my father's legacy. While unearthing his private files, I discovered that Bernard of Hollywood's Blondes took on a life of their own, monopolizing the Brunettes and Redheads in my father's archives. My mother and I (genetic redheads), accepted my father's obsession. What else could you do with a man who was known to the world as having discovered Marilyn Monroe — even if she wasn't "blonde all over"?

For nearly half a century, these gilded, radiant beings seduced my father's camera. Dancing to their own tune, and surrounded by luxurious furnishings, soft and sensuous furs, sheer and provocative gowns, and sexy swimsuits, the golden nymphs called out like sirens, "We are the flames of your fire."

Sheree North

"HAY THERE!"

Lisa Gibson

"TOP OF THE MORNING!"

Brigitte Bardot

"LOOK AT ME"

Lyn Mara

"UPSIDE-DOWN CAKE"

Marilyn Monroe

"SUMMER SMILE"

Jayne Mansfield

"SATIN LIPS"

Lili St. Cyr
"DON'T TOUCH!"

Lili St. Cyr

"FLAME"

Elli Marshall

"A SIP IN TIME"

Joy Lansing

"ISLAND DRESSING"

Jayne Mansfield

"KISSABLE"

Maila Nurmi

"LORELEI"

Neva Gilbert

"HI THERE!"

Reman

Lili St Cyr

"EARLY AMERICAN"

Berna

Norma Jean / Marilyn Monroe

"SHIP AHOY!"

Joyce Johnson

"POOLSIDE PIXIE"

Lili St.Cyr

"NEW HAT"

Dardy Orlando

"A STEP BEYOND"

Carolfae Petersen

"GONE SHOPPING"

June Dempsey

"HOLLYWOOD CALLING"

Irish McCullah

"JUNGLE HEAT"

Jane Powell

"PICTURE PERFECT"

Ava Norring

"GAMINE"

Jeanette Donnell

"WELL BALANCED"

Lili St.Cyr

"BUBBLE BATH"

Dardy Orlando

"WEDDING BELLE"

Barbara Nichols

"COLD OUTSIDE"

56

Corinne Calvet

"NIGHTY-NIGHT"

Many have contributed to making these publications possible: I am especially grateful to Bob Tabian, my agent, and my editor, Karen Kelly.

I owe special thanks to my assistant, Leslie Larson, and also Rod Vulich, Sygma photo agency, John Reichman, Mark Olbrich, Russell Adams, Theron Kabrich, John Gieo, London's Christie's, Ken Norwick, and my longtime legal guardian angel, Arthur Stashower.

Foremost, I am truly appreciative to my mother and father.